A Compass for the Classroom

*This book is dedicated to great teachers across the ages
who by their lives and struggles to find their way
have left us a trail to this compass.*

A Compass for the Classroom

How Teachers (and Students) Can Find Their Way & Keep From Getting Lost

Noah benShea   Robert C. DiGiulio

CORWIN PRESS
A Sage Publications Company
Thousand Oaks, California

For information:

Corwin Press
A Sage Publications Company
2455 Teller Road
Thousand Oaks, California 91320
www.corwinpress.com

Sage Publications Ltd.
1 Oliver's Yard
55 City Road
London EC1Y 1SP
United Kingdom

Sage Publications India Pvt. Ltd.
B-42, Panchsheel Enclave
Post Box 4109
New Delhi 110 017 India

Printed in the United States of America

Library of Congress Cataloging-in-Publication Data

BenShea, Noah.
A compass for the classroom : how teachers (and students) can find their way & keep from getting lost / Noah benShea, Robert C. DiGuilio.
    p. cm.
Includes bibliographical references.
ISBN 1-4129-0624-5 (cloth) — ISBN 1-4129-0625-3 (pbk.)
    1. Reflective teaching. 2. Effective teaching.
I. DiGiulio, Robert C., 1949- II. Title.
LB1025.3.B463 2005
371.102—dc22   2004013788

This book is printed on acid-free paper.

04   05   06   07   10   9   8   7   6   5   4   3   2   1

Acquisitions Editor:	Robert D. Clouse
Managing Editor:	Elizabeth Brenkus
Editorial Assistant:	Jingle Vea
Production Editor:	Diane S. Foster
Copy Editor:	Kristin Bergstad
Typesetter:	C&M Digitals (P) Ltd.
Proofreader:	Tracy Marcynzsyn
Cover Designer:	Tracy E. Miller
Graphic Designer:	Anthony Paular

Contents

About the Authors

Noah benShea is The Compass because he has—with wisdom, compassion, and humor—helped so many of us to find our way.

—Larry King, CNN

Noah benShea is a poet, philosopher, scholar, educator, humorist, lecturer, and international best-selling author who was, by the age of 23, an assistant dean of students at UCLA and, by 30, a consulting fellow to the esteemed long-range think-tank, The Center for the Study of Democratic Institutions in Santa Barbara, California. He has spoken at numerous universities, as well as given countless keynote addresses including to the Library of Congress. His work has been incorporated into publications of Oxford University and the World Bible Society in Jerusalem.

Often referred to as the "gurus' guru," he is the author of 16 books. Wide foreign sales for a number of his books continue a tradition begun with the *Jacob the Baker* series, which have been translated around the world and embraced as timeless fables in countries as diverse as China, Mexico, Spain, Italy, Brazil, Germany, Holland, Japan, Norway, and Israel, and were on the Korean Top 10 Best Sellers for six months where they sold more than 500,000 copies.

His insightful perspective on life is presented weekly in his online column, Noah's Window—www.noahswindow.com—which is carried globally via the Internet and by Noah's Window subscribers and speaks directly with hundreds of thousands of readers each week. Using the Internet's #1 search engine Yahoo! and the name "Noah benShea" we find more than 1,000 Web sites, including several foreign language Web sites, quoting from his speeches, books, and essays.

In 1999, he was nominated for the Grawemeyer Award for his presentation, "Ideas That Improve the World." From 1997 to 2002, his weekly essays were enjoyed by several million readers via the New York Times Newspaper Regional Network. And, in 1997, his weekly essays were nominated for a Pulitzer Prize.

"An Evening With Noah benShea" was nationally broadcast on PBS, and he has been widely interviewed on radio, television, and in print across North America. He has also had a daily "thought" feature on a regional ABC affiliate and a weekly radio talk show.

In addition to his reflective life, he was a founding partner and later chairman of a national manufacturing company. He is often called upon both for long-range forecasting and as an inspirational speaker to communities and companies. He has served on Boards of Directors and as a national lecturer to The Executive Committee, a business organization that counsels business men and women, and to a number of different branches of the Young President's Organization. He continues as an advisor to North American business and community leaders.

He is the father of a daughter, Jordan, and a son, Adam. Born in Toronto, Ontario, Canada, he lives in Santa Barbara, California. He can be reached at www.noahswindow.com andor noah@ noahswindow.com

 **Bob DiGiulio,** a lifelong teacher, is an education advocate as well as a Fulbright scholar and writer. He is professor of education at Johnson State College in Vermont. He earned his Ph.D. in human development from the University of Connecticut; he then earned his D.Ed. in socioeducation from The University of South Africa. A native Brooklynite, he began his teaching career in the inner-city New York City public schools, where he taught for a number of years. His career includes teaching at the elementary, middle, junior high, and college levels, ranging from crowded urban schools to a one-room schoolhouse, and he served as the principal of a school named a "School With Exemplary Discipline" by Ohio State University. As an educational consultant, he codeveloped Teen Test, a vocational counseling program for adolescents. He coauthored the educational software "Language Activities Courseware," and authored its teacher's guide. His *Teacher Magazine* article, "The 'Guaranteed' Behavior Improvement Plan," was recognized as having one of the highest total readership scores of any of that magazine's articles.

For about ten years, he worked as a counselor and speaker on parenting, and on coping with bereavement. He authored several books, notably *When You Are a Single Parent; Effective Parenting; Beyond Widowhood;* and *After Loss,* selected by *Reader's Digest* as one of their featured condensed books. His booklet *Losing Someone Close* has sold more than two million copies worldwide. He is a contributing author to *The Oxford Companion to Women's Writing in the United States* and *Marriage and Family in a Changing Society,* and is coauthor of *Straight Talk About Death and Dying.*

He has written several books for educators published by Corwin Press, including *Great Teaching; Educate, Medicate or Litigate?;* and *Positive Classroom Management.* He is a Life Member of the Fulbright Association, a member of the Peace Education Commission, American Educational Research

Association, and Kappa Delta Pi—International Honor Society in Education. He serves on Project Harmony's Advisory Board on Education Programs.

He is the father of four children and grandfather of three. He lives with his family in northern Vermont, and he can be reached at bob@digiulio.com

Men occasionally stumble over the truth, but most of them pick themselves up and hurry off as if nothing had happened.

—Sir Winston Churchill

PART I
A Compass for the Classroom

The Concept

1

A New Compass

Dear Reader . . .

Over the last number of years I have made several trips to Italy and, in particular, to a picturesque and historic region called the Amalfi coast. On one of the visits, in the town square of the small city of Amalfi, I came across the statue of Flavio Goia (Aczell, 2001), the man who, legend has it, was the father of the modern compass. And it got me thinking. And it got me doing some research in local libraries in my halting Italian. And it got me thinking further.

We have now had the benefit of a rather sophisticated compass for more than 500 years, and yet even now, so long after the invention of the compass, who among us has not felt lost in life or feared we were "losing it"?

Who among us has not felt afraid of losing our way in the day-to-day, or in the dark, or in love, or at work, or in growing up, or in growing older?

Who among us has not felt afraid of losing the company of others, or having only our own company, or wondering who could possibly want our company?

And how many among us have fears that we have lost our way or could lose our way in alcohol, or drugs, or gambling, or food, or in purchasing, or in pursuing success, or in the fear of failure?

Historically, in an attempt to find their way, people have turned from reading trail signs, to the stars, to maps, and eventually to a compass. And all of these methods have helped those who were lost find their way or stay on track. However, though most of us these days can tell north from south, we still need to find our way.

To that end, what you are about to read is of a new compass that can help any of us find our way and keep all of us from getting lost in all the ways that are not geographical.

But this is more than another self-help book in a me-first world. When I finished writing my book, *A Compass for Your Life*, one of the most trusted editors in the field of education, Robb Clouse, at Corwin Press, suggested I send the book along to Robert DiGiulio—a noted scholar and educator who had written many books that have helped teachers around the world in the classroom and in the transformation of their lives. Following on Mr. Clouse's advice of what he thought might be a great fit and of great service, I received a call from Dr. DiGiulio and an immediate respect and friendship was struck.

And while what you have in your hands now is a slim volume, it is more importantly a tool, a tool that will simply and fundamentally add leverage to all the other tools in your inventory. This tool is designed to help teachers find their own way in today's tumultuous world as well as to realize and rediscover the humanity, beauty, and joy of teaching. This is not a how-to-teach book, but a timeless ally to facilitate support and affirmation for teachers and their students in a time when those allies are hard to come by. If you will, here is a tool that in addition to all its other functions will also scrape today's tarnish off the most noble of professions. Here is *A Compass for the Classroom* that has the potential to serve you, your students, and your colleagues in untold ways. And we trust that you will lend others the Compass you find herein. *E grazie.*

—*Noah benShea*

2

Why We Need
a Compass

*Fear of being separated and becoming lost alone in the
jungle is a fear for all jungle infantrymen. Consequently,
every Army Ranger is taught how to navigate with a
compass—to move through impenetrable jungle to reach
a distant objective. A trained jungle soldier with a reliable
compass can get where he is heading. The self-confidence
felt by anyone alone in the jungle with a compass, that
they know how to use, has an importance hard to explain
to those lacking this experience.*

—U.S. Army Ranger Handbook

F ew of us are Army Rangers, and life is not a jungle, but
the jungle is part of life, and all of us are trying to find our
way through a dense tangle of characters, and questions, and
conflicts, and issues. All of us.

None of us have found our way who have not been lost.
Finding one's way is a work in progress and inevitably
requires the realization that the road ahead is always under
construction.

The ability to stay the course and keep our focus is how champions become champions. And this is tough work, even for champions. But finding our way is never as painful as being lost.

Knowing where we were yesterday may be reassuring, but it is not necessarily a path for finding our way tomorrow.

The best way to play the moment is to play the part and not the result. Life is an adventure. One of the most common ways of getting lost is when we live our life as a presumption and forget that the next moment in life is always uncharted territory.

Like all explorers across time who have wandered in uncharted territory, perhaps the most valuable ally we could have is something to help us chart our way.

To achieve this aim, our ancestors first studied the stars, and then drew maps, and then came up with the compass. The advantages of having a compass were manifold. The compass not only didn't rely on the stars, it didn't rely on our ability to see the stars. The compass also didn't take any special skill to operate, and, most important, it allowed one to take a sighting, travel a while, and then take another sighting to make sure one's path hadn't varied from one's goal.

The advent of the traditional compass was a huge leap in finding one's way. But the world has changed, and many of us who know where the sun rises and sets are still trying to find our way.

3

Why We Need a *New* Compass

You can't drive into the future staring into the rearview mirror.

Yesterday's solutions were solutions to yesterday's problems.

The problem today is that while all of us are trying to find our way with others, or ourselves, or with our work, or with our heart, few of us are lost geographically. Finding north, south, east, or west is not the directional quandary in most of our lives. How to find our way with others, or around others' issues, or to what matters most to us, these are our kind of compass needs and why we need a new compass.

To meet that need, you will soon read of four new and timeless Compass points that will absolutely help you find your way under any circumstances and with anyone.

4

Why We *All* Need a New Compass

To those who at the moment seem to be basking in success and wondering why they too need a new compass, a few thoughts:

Finding and losing our way emotionally, morally, philosophically, spiritually, and/or intellectually is not just something that happens on dark and stormy nights. And certainly not just something that happens to "others."

Whether we're rich or poor, the ability to become lost is an equal opportunity employer. Success on a bright and sunny day can be no less blinding than trying to operate in a blinding storm. All of us have, at some point, been in the dark—sometimes even at high noon.

Perhaps what's most important to remember is that all of us in life are in it together and need to be a compass for each other, even if both parties feel a little lost.

A man needed to begin a journey but the day had turned to night and he feared to begin. Unsure what to do the man turned to a sage in the community.

"Take someone with you," counseled the teacher.

"But," moaned the man, "if I do that then there will be two blind men on the path."

"No," said the teacher, "when two people discover each other's blindness it is already growing light" (benShea, 1990).

5

Instructions for People Who Don't Do Instructions

Years ago I watched my daughter tear open the wrapping on a birthday gift of a new camera. When I suggested she read the instructions, she told me, "I don't do instructions."

So, if you don't do instructions, here are a few, short things to keep in mind before you tear into how this new Compass works.

The new Compass is not a Magic 8 Ball, or a genie, or a fortune-teller. It is not intended to replace a commonsense tool like common sense, or a spiritual ally such as prayer. The Compass is rather a tool that adds leverage to all the other tools and allies in your inventory. And like any tool, it works once you learn how to use it. It won't take you long. It will take you a long way. And the right way.

By using this new Compass you will find a way—not only a way to help avoid mistakes, but also a way to mine your mistakes.

All of us living on planet Earth walk on a little blue ball spinning in space. All of us find our balance, and lose our balance, and find our balance, and. . . . The same is true with finding our way. It is not something that we solve. It is something we are always solving. All of us.

6

How the New Compass Works

It is not a philosopher's job to make simple things compli- cated but to make complicated things simple. And it is my hope that you will find the value of this new Compass is not in its complexity but in its simplicity.

The governing principles of the new Compass work on the same conditions of the traditional compass and here, too, the beauty is in the simplicity. The principle of the traditional compass is premised on a magnetized needle always pointing to magnetic north. It is only when we can establish what is magnetic north that we can establish what is east, south, or west.

Absent of magnetic north, east, south, or west have no meaning. They exist only as they exist in relationship. Without magnetic north, we are lost. And it is only when we can estab- lish north that we can find our way to anywhere we want to go geographically.

Similarly, with the new Compass we also have to begin with establishing where north is. Once we have done that, we can locate east, south, and west and keep from getting lost. But here is where the new Compass, borrowing on wisdom from all cultures and a lifetime of experience, makes a leap into a whole new way for finding our way.

On the new Compass, the four historic geographic directions are replaced with the following new directional markers:

North is replaced with Humility.

East is replaced with Honesty.

South is replaced with Love.

West is replaced with Faith.

Other than the changes you see on page 14, in every other way the new Compass works like the old compass.

If you wonder why this concept isn't more complicated, remember that there are only ten commandments and after thousands of years that's still enough to confound most of us. In life the obvious is often camouflaged by its obviousness.

The only difference between the new Compass and the old compass is that when any of us are trying to find our way with the new Compass, we begin not by finding north but by finding and taking a reading on our Humility.

From there we need to look to the new east, south, and west to see whether we are being honest, loving, and exercising faith.

Another way to envision this is as follows: Think of your eyes as a camera and each of the directions on the new Compass as a series of lenses that fit one on top of the other, each necessary for bringing the next into focus, each step in the sequence of lenses necessary to afford your vision more and more clarity so you can find your way and keep from getting lost. If one of the lenses is absent or dirty, your vision, the picture you see of the world—your world—will be absent or cloudy.

In any situation, facing any question, you can do no more than putting on the first lens and asking yourself

Am I being humble—not prideful—with myself, and my intentions, about myself, about my opinion, about my efforts, and with others?

From there you can put on the next lens and ask . . .

Am I being honest—or admitting when I'm not honest—with myself, and my intentions, and about my efforts, and with others?

From there you can put on the next lens and ask . . .

Am I being loving—passionate, and compassionate—to myself, and my intentions, and to my efforts, and to others?

And from there you can put on the next lens and ask . . .

Am I being faithful—patient in the day-to-day—with myself, and my intentions, to myself, to my efforts, and to others?

If you're into getting the news in a nutshell, that's the acorn—with one little reminder: From little acorns mighty oaks do grow.

7

The New Compass

Day to Day

While this Compass can help us answer life's toughest questions and biggest problems, most of us get caught in life's smallest moments, in day-to-day stuff. Indeed, it's often little things that make us see how small we can be. But whether it's life's big moments or everyday moments, this new Compass can be used to help us check ourselves along the way to make sure we're staying on the path we have in mind.

And because concepts like humility, honesty, compassion and passion, and patience and faith can be difficult real life day-to-day concepts, here are some Compass points in action, some things to remember to remind yourself along the way.

HUMILITY

We acknowledge that humanity has not yet reached its highest level. Admit this also about yourself. And you are already evolving, upward.

Admit when you are wrong.

Ask yourself why you can't admit it.

Don't insist on being right.

Ask yourself why you need to be right.

Admit when some aspect of your life is out of control and watch yourself take control.

Don't confuse being made in God's image with being God.

Don't exercise power just because you can.

All of us are from the Hand of God; none of us are the Hand.

Laugh when you trip over your own pride.

Openly admire the humility in others.

Embrace what you like least about yourself. Make it yours, and you will make it better.

Ask God how to mine your mistakes. Begin by mentioning them.

Do something nice for someone else, and don't tell anyone.

Stop confusing what you think with who you are.

Don't put off accepting yourself until you're perfect. Accept who you are for who you are now and you will be better off now, and have a better chance of being a better you in the future.

HONESTY

When you are born you are connected to your mother. When you are alive you are connected to Mother Earth. When you die your body dissolves into the universe. Death is only a change of cosmic address. You are a part of the whole. You know this. Do you live honestly believing this?

Don't lie to make people like you.

Don't trade kindness for honesty and think you've made an honest trade.

Say less. Only a quiet pond paints an honest picture.

Don't confuse that you can lie to yourself and be honest with others. All personal deceit will eventually lead to some form of social deceit.

Don't take credit just because credit lands in your lap.

Take a personal inventory. Count what you have. Count what's missing. Count yourself lucky. Give yourself a fair count.

Admit what is not flattering about you. And flatter yourself by admitting it.

To take a breath, we have to release our breath. Be honest about what no longer serves you and release it.

Observe your intentions and see how they line up against what you tell others is your intent.

Don't care about something because it is politically correct. Or think that in correcting others it necessarily makes you correct.

Admit to God what God already knows about you.

Find a mistake you can learn from. Reward yourself by finding another.

Admit to something even if it means you'll get less.

Admit to something you did just so others would think more of you.

Don't confuse being honest with not lying about money or sex. Be honest about lies in other areas of your life and why you lied.

Think about a time you told yourself you chose honesty over kindness in what you said to someone else. Was it honestly kindness or did it serve you more than protect another?

Think about whether what you say is bothering you is what's really bothering you, or are you telling yourself that because you can't admit to something else? And admit it.

LOVE

Love is made of passions and compassion. Passion alone has built buildings and burned them down. Be as passionate about caring for others as you are passionate about your passions.

Address someone you don't know as, "My friend."

Be passionate in what you choose as your passions.

What is something, or someone, you lusted for and told yourself you loved?

Give more than you get.

Let go of more than you take.

Release your hold on what is holding you back.

Be forgiving of someone even when you remember why you're angry with them.

Be prepared to chop wood to fuel your passion.

It is your work to make amends. It is not your work to see that things are finally mended.

Care when no one will reward you for it.

Don't see others as others.

See your vulnerability as a strength.

The Talmud reminds us: "Kindness is the highest wisdom." Be cautious of those who want to be wiser than caring. Be cautious of those who confuse kindness with weakness.

More than being giving, give a damn.

Visit someone who is sick, and don't tell anyone.

Give money to someone you don't know through someone you don't know.

Give someone back their anger without being angry.

The best measure of whether a society is civilized is how people with power treat people without power. When you're feeling powerful, do something civilized.

Observe when you have been so caring about something that you became uncaring about what your caring did.

Think of something you did in the past that saddened you and forgive yourself without giving yourself the right to do it again.

Think of something compassionate that happened to you but didn't seem like it was compassionate when it happened. Accept that your compassion for others won't always be seen as compassion, and be compassionate to yourself if you feel hurt.

No good deed goes unpunished, but that's not an excuse to avoid good deeds.

A fisherman is someone who cares less about what he catches and more about fishing. Play the part, not the result, in your life.

Good deeds are not a deal made with heaven.

Love yourself when you fail, and you will succeed.

FAITH

Faith and patience are difficult for the Occidental mind that feels if it isn't doing something it isn't doing. Often the most important thing we do in life is what we choose not to do. Sometimes there is nothing more important we can do than to let go and let God.

Wait your turn, in the supermarket line, in the parking lot, and when waiting for love.

Pray less "please" and more "thank you."

If you're waiting to hear from God, remember God may be waiting to hear from you. Be as impatient with yourself as you are with God. And you will learn patience.

Do something only on faith and if doesn't work out, do it again.

Tell a kid you believe in him or her. Tell them again.

Tell yourself the same thing.

Have patience with those you love. Remind yourself that you don't just love them in the moment but across time, and that across time they will need to have the same patience with you.

Knowing we are less gives us room to become more. Humility is the first door you must pass through to get to faith. Humility leads to faith. Let yourself be led there.

Prayer is not room service. God is not a cosmic bellhop.

God does make house calls if you invite God into your home.

Admit to yourself when you talk about having faith in God but lose your patience with people. Have patience with yourself on this issue.

Think about something that happened after you had done everything you could, and nothing happened, and you felt nothing would. Remember this.

Remember that God isn't done with you yet, and you are a work of art but a work in progress. And others are too.

Remember that sometimes the fastest way to get somewhere is to put on the brakes.

When you are in a hurry, go slowly.

Hope for the best; make peace with the rest.

The best way to make it through the day is to remember you only have to make it through one day at a time. Every day.

Do everything you can to make something you really want to happen, happen. Do it humbly, honestly, passionately and compassionately, and then turn away, and be patient. And patient for a little longer yet.

Life can be an unexpected joy. Expect that. Faith sees around corners.

8

May You Go From Strength to Strength

I t is said that a politician thinks about the next election and a leader thinks about the next generation. When I wrote *A Compass for Your Life* I meant it as a Compass for all of us. In this book, *A Compass for the Classroom*, that intention is honored in a manner beyond even my best intentions because teachers are leaders and influence generations.

In the pages that follow, every teacher and, through every teacher, every student has the opportunity to find their way and keep from getting lost.

If my work has been a candle against the night, I feel blessed. And in having Dr. DiGiulio's remarkable application of *A Compass for the Classroom* just ahead of you, you are fortunate for this lantern.

Teacher to teacher, it is my wish that you go from strength to strength and be a source of strength to others.

Pssst! Take a Compass.

PART II

A Compass for the Classroom

The Application

9

A Compass to Guide Teachers

Sometimes, life presents us with an unexpected and remarkable confluence of events. Robb Clouse, the Acquisitions Editor at Corwin Press, contacted me several months ago. Robb told me of a renowned author he knew whose style might blend well with mine, leading to our possible collaboration on a book for educators. Robb said his name was Noah benShea. I smiled at the coincidence, because only a few days earlier I had purchased several books to use in my teacher education classes. One of the books was Noah's *Jacob the Baker*. Since I teach a graduate course on the philosophies of education, I wanted to find a work by a contemporary Western author that reflected the Idealist philosophy—a philosophy that holds that truth is eternal and unchanging, and that knowledge and truth lie within us, needing only to be brought out. Referring to the teaching ability of Socrates, Plato said that the good teacher is a "midwife of ideas." The good teacher does not pump information into a student, but helps lead knowledge—which is already there—out of the student, mostly through skillful questioning. Plato tells of an ignorant slave boy who showed he knew advanced mathematics, his knowledge "given birth" through the teaching skills of his excellent teacher, Socrates.

With similar skill, in *Jacob the Baker,* Noah's title character Jacob brings out wisdom in people around him, even as he shuns personal fame and tributes. Jacob himself speaks with much wisdom, yet with deep humility, because he is constantly aware of the Source of wisdom. Like the very best of teachers, Jacob does not have all or even most of the answers. But what he does have is the very best of questions, which help his villagers find Truths within themselves.

Hence, I was delighted to speak with Noah about his Compass, agreeing that it could be used as a tool to help teachers, educators, and even parents find their way in a world grown quite distant from its inner self; a world confusing with its countless rules and laws, dizzying consumer choices, and insoluble crises. I found Noah to be, in many ways, a mirror of Jacob, for just as Jacob wrote phrases of simple humanity and wisdom into his breads, Noah has done just that with his books. So the answer was, "Yes, absolutely." I told Robb that I'd be honored to collaborate with Noah.

This collaboration was exciting to me in one other way. Previous to this work, I had written 11 books on the subjects of teaching, parenting, and recovery from loss. My books tend to be cognitive, practical, and answer-oriented, and until this collaboration with Noah, I had not had much opportunity to speak to the inside-educator: the level at which teachers are *real.* In a profession that has been buffeted by demands, pushes, and pulls, the Compass allows us teachers to *place ourselves back within the process of teaching and learning,* by guiding us toward becoming *truly highly qualified teachers, qualified not by test scores but by caring, teaching skill, and wisdom.* As such, the Compass allows us to recognize the oldest truths of Idealism, and to apply them to teaching today, in the modern world. Good teaching is still good teaching; as it was in Socrates' time, so it is today. Each of our students today is as gifted as Socrates' slave boy, awaiting only a good teacher to bring out his or her gifts. In a similar way, the Compass is a "good teacher" guide for educators, a guide that helps illuminate the gifts that are already within each of us. These gifts are the Compass points of Humility, Honesty, Love, and Faith.

So in addition to all the people I wish to thank, my sincere appreciation goes to Robb Clouse for being the perceptive matchmaker, and one whose vision and expertise have brought to life many fine and useful books for educators worldwide. Also, of course, I thank my collaborator Noah benShea, who is a midwife in the best Idealist tradition. I appreciate not only his origination of the Compass and many wise writings, but also his willingness to share his wonderful concept in a way that benefits others. As teachers who use the Compass will learn, the Compass helps us through each of our labors. As a result, we find the baby to be quite beautiful.

—Bob DiGiulio

10

Why a Compass for the Classroom?

These are uncertain times for all of us humans, and teachers are no exception. Given the nature of the job of teaching, today's uncertainties present particular challenges for teachers. For instance, with today's push to hold schools accountable, standardized test scores are used as indicators of student success or failure, and schools and teachers are also being evaluated by the same data. As a result of this emphasis on test scores, the skills and qualities of good teaching become less obvious, because no short-answer, multiple-choice exam can measure—and thus draw attention to—those skills and qualities. Good teachers feel their roles are becoming more scripted as they are pressured to teach to a test, with a resulting de-emphasis on creativity and spontaneity. Meeting individual students' needs is made more difficult to do in a test-driven environment. As a result of this accountability frenzy, schools place greater emphasis on *training* students to recall the right answers, with a diminished emphasis on critical thinking and problem solving. In 1953, eastern philosopher and teacher Jiddu Krishnamurti warned that, "Education is not merely a matter of training the mind. Training makes for efficiency, but it does not bring about completeness. A mind that has merely been trained is the continuation of the past, and such a mind can never discover the new." As a result of today's definition of education-as-training, teachers (and students) are being short-circuited, held back from what their *center* tells them is most important about learning and growth.

Fortunately, we now have *A Compass for the Classroom*, a tool that turns attention toward what is really important in teaching and learning. *A Compass for the Classroom* works directly at that *center*, speaking to where our mind and heart need to go, and grow. Because it addresses *qualitative aspects* of teaching, and speaks to the humanity of each teacher and student, *A Compass for the Classroom* refocuses attention away from the didactic and quantitative, and *toward the heart of good teaching*.

Ms. Smith exemplifies such a teacher. When my daughter was in seventh grade, she had a teacher she absolutely adored—my daughter's schoolwork improved, her home-work was done well, and handed in on time, plus she was far more positively inclined toward going to school, even despite the itchiness inherent in being a young adolescent. Why? Because my daughter believed that Ms. Smith liked her, and she liked the other kids, too. Plus, Ms. Smith trusted my daughter and the class, and made the students feel that their work and their contributions and ideas were *important, good,* and *valuable*. Ms. Smith did not emphasize mindless confor-mity or busy-work, but was an enabler for her students. My daughter told me, "Dad, Ms. Smith is a *real teacher* (emphasis hers). She is how a teacher is supposed to be!"

Second, we need *A Compass for the Classroom* because many teachers are isolated—physically, socially, and professionally—especially in today's large, larger, and gargantuan school cam-puses. Principals, deans, and department chairs who used to personally provide professional direction and support for teachers are occupied—if not preoccupied—by their own responsibilities. Some are overwhelmed and do not have much time to spend in classrooms with teachers and students. A few do not know the names of teachers within their own schools. Thus, many teachers are missing important support and affirmation for what they do. By itself, *A Compass for the Classroom* cannot replace human affirmation, but it does provide an important *tool* or *touchstone* for personal reflection, and it fosters reflective conversation among teachers, between teachers and administrators, and among teachers, administrators, and students. *A Compass for the Classroom* provides teachers with a *vocabulary: a language to describe what teachers do that is essential to student success.*

Finally, we Americans value individuality, choices, and doing our own thing. "Looking out for number one" has resulted in business productivity, yet teaching and learning remain social, cooperative enterprises, not a competitive undertaking. What are best practices for managers and customers of McDonald's and Burger King are not necessarily good practices for schools, teachers, or students. Teachers need collegiality, and mutual support to be successful. Trying to outdo each other is not helpful to teachers and students as it is in, say, banking, baseball, or bike racing. On the contrary: Teachers who *do not compete but work together* create successful students. This compass lends itself perfectly to individual self-realization, but also to collaboration among teachers. In sum, *A Compass for the Classroom* facilitates support, direction, and affirmation, and it also can form the centerpiece of high quality professional development for teachers.

A Compass for the Classroom helps students as well. Studies have looked at resilient young persons, those who survive under the most difficult of home and life circumstances, usually involving abuse and neglect. A critical factor as to whether or not such children will survive psychologically, emotionally, and even physically is the *presence or absence of at least one significant adult;* someone—and it takes only one—who thinks the child is special and values the child for being special. Sometimes this adult is the child's parent, but often it is not. In many cases it is a teacher, a person seen by troubled children as the only adult in the world who understands and accepts them for themselves. Renowned educator and author

Herbert Kohl (1994) said that there are teachers who look past the outward hostility that some young persons show toward the world, and "reach beyond the resistance" to connect with that child or adolescent. These special teachers are not easily pushed away by the child's behavior or attitude, as almost all other adults are. Even looking at the so-called normal population of students, researchers have pointed to the tremendous importance of teachers in this sense: Teachers not as ones making students memorize lots of information, but teachers as ones who establish and maintain a positive connection with a child. Through the transformed Compass points of Humility, Honesty, Love, and Faith, the teacher has all he or she needs to help students grow in healthy and prosocial ways, and to establish and nurture that caring connection.

11

What a Compass for the Classroom Provides

The Compass speaks to the *scope* and *quality* of the teacher-student relationship. On one hand, the Compass provides a personal guide to being one's best teacher, being one's best self. To borrow from one of Noah benShea's books, "No one ever became a better teacher or a better anything who wasn't working on also being a better person." By speaking to touch points in our teacher-selves, the Compass points help teachers gain direction, set priorities, plan for lessons, assess wisely, and set long-term goals for our students and our selves. In a sense, the points help us keep our finger on the pulse of our teaching. In addition, they provide a *means of communication* between student and teacher, and among teachers and administrators. Taken together, the four Compass points provide a common language and a way to talk about—and act on—what is most important in our professional lives, our students' lives, and the life of our classroom and school.

The world is far from an ideal place to live. Especially today, young people see the world as a dangerous place, a phenomenon called the Mean World Syndrome. But that is *precisely* the reason why teachers and classrooms are so essential: Teachers can create a safe, caring, and robust classroom society, where students can safely learn, and learn how to treat others. The Compass is the map for that to come about.

These days, all teachers need a Compass. Experienced teachers and new teachers, student teachers and master teachers find themselves pondering what is most important for us to do as teachers. Which endeavors should receive our focus and efforts? In the points of the Compass below are listed "component statements" for each Compass point. Each set of statements is a representative list of manifestations of that Compass point's essential features. These component statements are useful signposts, and are followed by illustrations, ways to your Compass point. We will address these statements and illustrations later in the book, when we try to help you see your areas of strength, and areas that could be strengthened.

12

Points of the Compass

On every compass are four main points: north, east, south, and west, and on every compass, the needle always points to magnetic north. The other directions—west, east, and south—exist in relation to north. Without magnetic north we lose our bearing, and our sense of direction. Just as the three other main compass points rely on their relationship to north, so too is it the case with *A Compass for the Classroom*, for which the fundamental point is *Humility*. Like true north, Humility constitutes the *raison d'etre* for teachers and teaching itself. To a teacher, magnetic north points to *what is best for students. How can my students be successful as learners—and as human beings?*

NORTH: TOWARD HUMILITY

If I am not for myself then who will be for me?

But, if I am only for myself, what am I?

And, if not now, when?

—Hillel

For teachers, **Humility** means *placing students' needs first.* It is the ultimate act of humility for teachers to look outside themselves and grasp the needs of other humans. Equating humility with humanity, Turkish scholar Fethullah Gulen (2004) speaks of humility as a sign that people have "become truly human," and that humility means we have a firm sense of our humanity, which does not get altered by a change in our wealth, learning, status, or fame. If those factors do change us, then we have not attained true humility or true humanity. Hence, Humility is the main Compass point for teachers, because it describes the connection of teachers to their humanity, their sense of being human within themselves. Humility is activated through teachers' relationships to others, that is to say, through their modeling truly human behavior.

Like good doctors who are dedicated to their patients' physical well-being ("above all do no harm"), the good teacher sees students' academic and social well-being as his or her first priority. But teachers have an even greater burden than doctors, for they must do more at every turn than "doing no harm." Teachers cannot—as doctors can sometimes do—decide to do nothing and allow an "educational immune system" to work its cure. No, teachers must continually be pro-active, doing what is good for students.

Guiding Statements of Humility

In my role as a teacher, I

Am here for my students, and not vice-versa. "I teach students, not subjects."

Think about, plan for, and teach to what will be beneficial for my students. If I am wrong or off the mark, I will change it for next time.

Involve students in planning, and in the life of the classroom. I'm not fearful of sharing power with my students, and believe it is necessary in order for them to take responsibility for their learning and growth.

Simplify myself, my teaching, my students' lives.

Am able to admit when I am wrong. I can apologize.

Am prepared for my classes, but never so rigidly that I cannot digress from my plans to take advantage of teachable moments. I'm open to many wonderful things that can happen in a classroom that no lesson plan can predict.

Am "God's gift"? Of course! I am not perfect, but like all good teachers, I am part of the multitude of God's gifts to humanity, and I honor that by working each day to become the best teacher possible. I am not falsely modest; my seeking to become a great teacher is ultimately a benefit to others, to my students. False modesty has no place here. To denigrate my worth as a teacher serves only to denigrate my students.

Use my power as a teacher wisely and with modesty, working gently, but resolutely.

Provide human affirmation for myself, my colleagues, and my students. The human factor is essential. I like to say that "true joy—and good teaching—cannot be measured by arithmetic."

The Compass Point of Humility in Practice

No matter how young or old your students may be, they must be included in the life of the classroom. In other words, good teaching means establishing a trusting give-and-take with students, where they can express their ideas, interests, and preferences. This means that those expressions are taken seriously by teachers. The point of Humility allows teachers to accept students' thoughts and feelings, not out of mere courtesy, but with joy. Of course, this demands much of the teacher. He or she must set the initial tone very early in the school year, showing the way for students individually and collectively to express themselves clearly but respectfully. The best way for teachers to do this is to *model* the behavior, instead of merely reciting rules. In fact, it's worth the time at the start of the term to devote a goodly portion of the day to discussing, modeling, practicing, and reviewing ways to relate to each other that are productive.

Teachers who actively model humility pass up the chance to assert their ego in order to recognize the needs of others.

The payoff comes when students imitate this teacher-behavior, out on the playground, at home, or in their out-of-school friendships with other students and neighborhood friends. They will themselves be teachers.

I try to give my students choices whenever it is possible, and I try to give them a real say in what their day will look like. Our field trip was almost totally planned by my (sixth-grade) students. When we returned, they visited the other classes in our school, telling them all about what they had learned. My students seemed even more charged up by this teaching experience than by the trip itself! Being able to teach what they had learned to other students and teachers really reinforced what they had learned.

Humility tempers us, too. Persistence is important for teachers, but it has its limits. Ms. C reminds us that sometimes we teach best when, for example, we cut short a lesson that is not working out. In a real way, it teaches our students that we are *human*. This realization can bring a class and a teacher wonderfully close; time is better spent in discussion than in plowing on, full speed ahead, through a lesson that has gone awry. Ms. C recalled:

> My algebra lesson went wrong from the start. I was confusing the x and y axes as I wrote on the board; some knew right away, and a few were giggling. Then I realized I had photocopied the wrong practice problems. I decided right there to draw the lesson to an end, and start fresh tomorrow morning. As it turned out, the review discussion we had in place of that algebra lesson was really helpful for my students. Sometimes you have to admit to a total malfunction and pick up the pieces as best you can!

Mr. D's Humility showed through an interaction he had with a Korean American student in his mostly Hispanic New York City classroom. Mr. D explains:

> In my first year of teaching in an inner-city public school, I graded students' papers and handed them back, having

written comments on them in red ink. One of my students seemed distressed with her paper. Hesitantly, she pointed to her name, which I had written into my comments. She said, "In Korea, when you write somebody's name in red, that person may soon die." Horrified, I told her, "Hei, you are a wonderful student!" I apologized for alarming her, and threw away my red pen. She seemed relieved, and I was too. Since that day I use only green ink to grade student work.

Modesty about what we are doing as teachers means that we are aware that we cannot possibly teach our students all—or even most—of what they need to know, and will need to know, in their lives. In his classic work *How Children Fail,* John Holt (1964) said

Since we cannot know what knowledge will be most needed in the future, it is senseless to try to teach it in advance. Instead, we should try to turn out people who love learning so much and learn so well that they will be able to learn whatever needs to be learned.

Finally, a marvelous lesson in Humility was offered recently when a beloved Bangor, Maine, elementary teacher, Karen Achorn-Ingalls, died unexpectedly (Ordway, 2004). Her last lesson had been a science lesson using plastic cups filled with pebbles and plastic cups filled with table salt. After first predicting which would be heavier, her students were surprised to discover that the cup filled with the salt was lighter in weight than the cup with pebbles. After Ms. Achorn-Ingalls died, principal Janet McIntosh went to each of her classes to help students cope with their teacher's death. She used the same cups, pebbles, and salt to build on the teacher's science lessons:

I told them the pebbles were life's blessings and that blessings happened every day. But then I showed them the cup of salt and I told them that even in a life full of blessings there comes some sadness and loss and that was what the salt represented. I hung the pebbles on the scale and then I hung the cup of salt on the scale and I tried to show them how life's blessings always outweighed the losses. I had hidden a pebble inside the salt and afterward I dug the pebble out of the salt and told them that even in times of sadness and loss you can sometimes find a little blessing.

EAST: TOWARD HONESTY

To make your children capable of honesty is the beginning of education.

—John Ruskin

For teachers, Honesty means *valuing truthfulness both in yourself and in your students.* There are many paths to improvement as a teacher, but every path requires honest self-appraisal. The very best, experienced teachers know they developed their skills and qualities over time, and only after honest reflection.

Guiding Statements of Honesty

In my role as a teacher, I

Believe—truly believe—all my students can—and will— be successful.

Treat all my students fairly. I ask questions of all; I involve all students.

Trust my good judgment far more than other measures or tests given to my students.

Teach my students that their own self-assessments of their work are even more essential than institutional assessments of their work.

Am honestly successful as a teacher, yet I have no apologies for that success because that is my job and my calling. *I am successful because I work at it; I work at it because I love teaching people.*

Reflect with honesty upon my teaching, seek to change what must be changed, and keep what works well.

Dialogue with my colleagues in a reflective way.

Encourage students to speak up for justice, and not just when their self-interest or self-convenience is at stake.

Give students opportunities to revise their work, to do it over without penalty. This teaches them, *There is no endpoint to learning.*

Provide clear and honest feedback to students, and teach them to do the same with self-feedback and feedback on other students' work. I seek to go beyond simple praise (*"Good work," "Super"*), and provide feedback that is more specific, and informative ("Yes, you remembered to capitalize all the proper nouns!").

Never fear sharing my enthusiasm with my students, and never prevent students from sharing their enthusiasm with me and the class.

Monitor students' work over time. Like ships passing through locks in a canal, my students get support along the way so that failure is quite impossible.

Encourage students to self-monitor. They could keep a journal, for example, and chart their thoughts, hopes, progress, setbacks, helping them to see their own Compass points.

Can be relied upon to keep confidential information.

Use good assessments to help inform my instruction. All good assessments help us see where to go; they are compasses unto themselves.

The Compass Point of Honesty in Practice

What can be more honest than sharing enthusiasm? The late Fred Rogers, host of television's *Mister Rogers' Neighborhood*, exemplified a teacher who emanated enthusiasm. A gentle man, Fred Rogers looked directly at the viewer, and spoke in a personal way to his audience. He told children how special they were: How there is only one person in the whole world who is "just like you, and that is you." His shows consisted of a variety of experiences of interest to children, all of which were infused with his brand of warm enthusiasm. This helped forge a connection between himself and others. Mr. Rogers would have made a great elementary teacher.

In the inner-city schools of Baltimore is a teacher I'll call "Mr. J." A dynamic middle-grades teacher, Mr. J also emanates enthusiasm, although he couldn't appear to be more different from Fred Rogers. Mr. J is a young African American male, an inner-city teacher of the most challenging of students. Like Mr. Rogers, his enthusiasm for young people is infectious, although Mr. J describes what he relishes in words quite different from those of Mr. Rogers:

The principal puts the (violent) student in my room. Because I appear to have the ability to deal with the most difficult students in the school. Yes, I am a male, but it is my vision for students that is different. . . . I love difficult students; my satisfaction is that if you can move a child from A to B, not only in mathematics and reading and science, but in behavior, then you are successful. For if you cannot change social behavior, it is more difficult to change academic behavior.

Honesty is a tough call in 21st-century America. For what does it mean to be truthful in a culture that emphasizes winning, sometimes at any cost? On the other hand, must truthfulness compel us to acknowledge and/or reveal to students what may not be flattering about ourselves or in our best interests? Not necessarily, and it may even be less-than-honest to emphasize our weak points as humans and as teachers, particularly since they may serve to diminish us in the eyes of our students, and/or elicit their pity. Should we show our humanity? Of course. Should we be real? Always. But our students are not well served to see us in every possible hue; certainly not as victims or martyrs. On the other hand, being honest with our students demands that we show students what is wonderful about us; for example, our wisdom, kindness, fairness, and on and on. We teach these best not through our words or demands, but through our actions, our activity, and our preparation for teaching. This tells students they are worth our time, and we are worth their time and attention. Nancy Hottinger, 2002 European Area District Teacher of the Year (U.S. Department of Defense, 2002), places her highest emphasis on teacher honesty:

If a teacher hypocritically demands perfection from students, all the while exhibiting laziness and lack of preparation, the young people will not be fooled. In fact, they will lose their essential respect for the teacher and the learning mission will be compromised.

Give your own tests, and trust in the value of your own good judgment. A teacher's assessments of students' work are by far the most valid and reliable measure of student learning. No test, standardized or otherwise, can replace the good judgment of a teacher:

> I was working with Brad, my student teacher, and told him he needed to come up with ways to assess what the students had learned following his lesson. No store-bought test could give Brad that information. Plus, he needed to guide the students toward self-assessment. Brad told the other student teachers that he didn't know what I wanted him to do. When I learned this, at our seminar the student teachers and I brainstormed many types of assessment strategies that gave us good information about our students. Within two minutes, they named 11 assessment strategies student teachers (and Brad) could use in place of standardized tests: portfolios, silently observing students as they worked, student-teacher conferences, student-to-student conferencing, classwide experience summaries, student presentations, individual and group projects, quizzes, having students make up questions, keeping journals and logs, and teacher-made tests.

Ms. W, a Connecticut middle school teacher, offers more suggestions that speak to the point of Honesty:

> When students have a due date for an assignment, remind them prior to the due date, and ask how much progress they have made so far. . . . I don't allow failure in my classroom. You have to work extremely hard in my class to flunk. It's a lot easier to work hard in my room and do well than it is to work extremely hard in order to flunk.

One of the strongest statements of honesty is when teachers openly acknowledge a student's differences to the class. In the case of students with disabilities who are mainstreamed into the regular classroom, teachers who honestly and directly explain to the class that, for example, Jason is hearing-impaired, thus he could benefit from students who want to help him, are exemplifying the point of Honesty. To the benefit of all, Jason's teacher taught her enthusiastic class American Sign Language, which opened up a channel of good communication among the students. Even away from Jason, students signed to each other! Jason's teacher's high-profile, frank, and honest exposition of his disability helped Jason be well regarded, never lacking a partner during work, lunch, or recess times.

SOUTH: TOWARD LOVE

Only learning that is enjoyed will be learned well.

—Judah Ha-Nasi, in Gribetz (1997)

For teachers, Love means *accepting students unconditionally.* Teachers do not have to *like* each of their students. This would be a super-human expectation. But teachers must *love* every one of their students. That is a basic expectation.

Guiding Statements of Love

In my role as a teacher, I

Know my students by name; I know them as people, as outside-of-class individuals.

Respect my students' parents and families, and their cultural traditions, norms, and values.

Love even students who act up or who are unpleasant or rude to me or to others. *My love is unconditional; I will change students' behavior by teaching them, and not by rejecting or not loving them.*

Guard students' dignity in my classroom; I teach all my students how to safeguard their dignity and how to protect the dignity of others.

Avoid harshness and punitive measures. Yes, students respond to threats, but they never learn when fearful. They simply comply until the threat passes.

Look at students when I speak to them and attune my mind to what they are saying.

Orient students toward each other. Students should freely choose their friends from among classmates, but they must never treat others in an unloving or unkind way.

Teach students to reflect on something good that took place in their day, a joyful moment, perhaps, for their journal.

Actively plan for incorporating something joyful into my teaching. Sharing joy and enthusiasm will produce far better results than other methods.

The Compass Point of Love in Practice

Mr. J offers an example of how he modeled positive behavior in a situation where a student sought to insult him:

I was teaching conflict resolution to my class. I was teaching them how to nullify a negative statement. They were very excited about it. I told them of how I was walking by the junior high school, and this young girl looked at me and said, "You are so ugly!" And I responded, "Thank you!" She said, "Why did you say 'thank you'?" I said, "Because you look at a person being ugly as a negative, but I thought you looked at me so long before you concluded that I was ugly." And by using a negative statement I could become positive, and that moves them (the students).

Students themselves say that teachers show caring for students through the way teachers look at, listen to, and treat students, and how students feel understood. But perhaps even more, teachers show caring by the way they focus on student learning and uphold expectations for students, both for their schoolwork and their behavior. Ms. R is an example of a teacher who holds high expectations for students:

I have a reputation for being tough but fair. If you're fair, respect them and allow them to have their say you will be successful. I start each day by saying "good morning," "good afternoon." The students say, "You're the only teacher who speaks this way, who expects us to respect each other."

Just as people learn aggressive behavior through modeling (as in the vicious circle of child abuse, where abusive adults are usually those who were abused as children), consistent exposure to caring, loving adult behavior results in students modeling those caring, loving behaviors. Students learn powerfully when teachers are caring. In fact, research indicates that minority group students respond especially well to caring behaviors by teachers. A high school student told me

How do I know Ms. Johnson cares about us? She talks to us. She is interested in what we do outside of school. She doesn't judge us on our schoolwork. She notices when we get a hair cut, or when we are not feeling good. She doesn't get nervous, or try to rush me when I talk to her like some other teachers do. I think the most important thing about Ms. Johnson is that she makes me feel—makes us feel—that we are important.

All humans have a basic need to be loved. This is true with romantic relationships, but it is equally true in social situations, like school. Students must first feel they are loved before they can move ahead to get higher-level needs met. Feeling safe is a prerequisite to feeling loved. In fact, the most powerful love-building teaching strategy begins with establishing a safe classroom environment, providing an opportunity for students to share and witness appropriate ways to reply to others. A well-regarded local middle grades teacher opens each class with a structured sharing time, where students take turns talking and listening, deeply involved in questioning, probing, laughing, and adding to the contributions of other classmates.

Of course, teachers are also key people in helping students get their higher-level needs met. Those needs include an appreciation of mathematics, art, music, science, as well as languages, and social relationships. Indeed, higher-level needs involve the four Compass points themselves: Student appreciation of Humility, Honesty, Love, and Faith.

A teacher's Compass point of Love of her students can be a most powerful educational tool. I remember my fourth-grade teacher as if it were only yesterday. Sister Dolores made an impact on me that has carried on more than 40 years of my life. She made me feel special; she made it clear to me that I was an important member of our class. For example, one day she changed my seat, placing me next to Steven, a very troubled boy. Smiling, she whispered to me, "I hope some of you will rub off on Steven. You are a good example for him." In response to her kindness and belief in my goodness, and her love, I decided I loved her as well, and would do anything to please her. Years later, at my 35th high school reunion, I was talking to several alumni, classmates who became successful in a variety of professions and trades. When I mentioned Sister Dolores to them, several classmates who had also been students in her classroom became animated, telling me how they also loved Sister. Each had an affirming story, similar to my memory of being seated next to Stephen. We realized we each felt the same love for her, due to the same gift she shared with us. We saw the durable power of that wonderful teacher. Sister helped each of us believe in ourselves; that we were good, and worthwhile persons. She made each of us her special student, yet without making us special at the cost of another student being diminished. In her eyes, we weren't *relatively* special, but *absolutely* special. Sister's unconditional love for each of us was a powerful testimonial to her Compass point of Love.

WEST: TOWARD FAITH

Faith is the substance of things hoped for, the evidence of things not seen.

—Hebrews 11:1

For teachers, Faith means *teaching students to believe in themselves and others as a way of honoring all of God's creations.* Each student—each human being—is potentially his or her own best teacher. Through Faith we see that if we offer our students what is beautiful, mysterious, affirming, and marvelous about learning, they will freely choose to pursue those ends. When they are able to do so (through our modeling and encouragement), and given the freedom to do so, students serve as their own best teachers. With the Compass point of Faith, there is no need for teachers to plead, punish, threaten, or implore. *After all, my students and I are one. When students hurt, teachers hurt. When they are joyful, we smile.*

Guiding Statements of Faith

In my role as a teacher, I

Use my power to empower students, so they can be in charge of their own learning, and ultimately, themselves. This is the best gift I can give my students.

Hold clear but reasonable expectations for my students to achieve, and do all I can to facilitate that.

Believe all students can be—*and will be*—successful in my classroom.

Teach students about their role in being successful.

Work at becoming a better listener . . . and a lesser talker: I aim to have my students talk more than I do. My best assets are my ears and my face; they are my "show and tell": My ears—our ears—*show* students we are listening to what they are saying; My smiles—our smiles—*tell* students we like what we are hearing.

Teach my students how to listen to each other, and to themselves, which helps develop each student's "inner teacher."

Am a teacher, not a judge. Passing out verdicts, rulings, and sentences has little educational value.

Accept my students for who they are, today, right now.

Teach students to understand *attributions;* reasons for their success or failure in school.

Know that a teacher's disengaged, *laissez-faire* approach to students can destroy Faith fairly quickly.

Trust my students and show that trust by my behavior.

The Compass Point of Faith in Practice

In our modern technological society, it has become simpler to avoid fundamentally human ways of interacting with each other, ways that define us as human. Look at truth, which is central to the point of Faith. As an illustration, your school may have a policy that students must bring a written excuse for all absences. Fine, but try to not let that institutional policy define all of your person-to-person dealings with your students. Instead of the "Two-forms-of-picture-identification-please" approach, try to give priority to the *words* of your students, rather than doing so only when their words can be corroborated. For instance, and especially with middle school and high school students, don't demand verification of everything they tell you. Allow yourself to trust *they routinely tell you the truth.* Tell your students you will take what they tell you as truth. They may not always adhere to truthfulness, but your being suspicious and trying to prevent them from telling an untruth will fail; your demanding corroboration will never help students become more truthful or trustworthy. When Ann, one of my college students, missed a class, she said, "I had a dental appointment. Do you want a note from the dentist to prove I went?" I replied, "No, no note. *Your word* is good enough for me."

Faith means believing in students, and in their capacity to work independently. Don't confuse expecting students to be responsible for their own work (very valuable) with a disinterested, disengaged *laissez-faire* teaching approach. Nor should we think that helping students succeed involves doing too much for them. Guiding students toward success is not the same as spoon-feeding them. In some circumstances, spoon-feeding is an appropriate teaching strategy: My son-in-law patiently guided me step-by-step in using my computer's new digital scanner; my daughter taught me in the same way how to use a cell phone properly (without inadvertently dialing random, stored phone numbers!). In school, Faith helps teachers get close to students, monitoring and supporting their success, without feeling put-upon or worried that we teachers are doing too much for students. Mr. T says

Except when there is a test, I always give my students time to check their answers with a partner. I find that this helps them listen to each other, and really raises the quality of the work they do. They are less dependent on me, and more self-dependent.

There is enormous power built into the practice of *attributing*. In fact, the most empowering and Faith-building strategy a teacher can use is *attributing*. Attributing is a way of assessing students' work, then giving students affirming feedback that guides students toward continued success. Attributing means teaching students the *reasons for their success (or failure)*. Attributing teaches students *to be aware of what they did that caused success.* For example, "Angela, you did really well on that book project, but you know, I saw you reading lots of books. Your hard work paid off!" Or, "I noticed that you work hard in math, keep it up!"

Attributing is a lot better than *coercing*—telling students what they *should* have or *should not* have done. Teachers mean well when they say, "Given your ability, you should be a better reader." Or, "You passed the test, but with your ability you should've gotten an 'A.'" These comments may be intended as motivators, but they never feel very motivating to the recipient, who reasons, "I passed the test but I should have gotten an 'A,' I'm told. Thus, since I'm told I have a lot of ability, my poor showing was due to . . . laziness? Or maybe I'm just not as smart as they think I am?" Coercing is unhelpful in guiding students to develop their Compass.

My sixth-grade teacher told my mom that I was doing well, but that I was an "underachiever." Hmmm . . . I didn't know what to do about *that*. Neither did my parents, who felt bad to hear this. All they could do was urge me to put forth more effort. It would have been far more helpful had my teacher not labeled me, but helped me out of that situation. We could've started, perhaps, by my doing more than munching through mindless worksheets. Years later, when I was a school principal, I urged my teachers to provide for meaningful schoolwork, and never to let the word "underachiever" cross their lips! The way to help students put forth more effort is through *motivation*, and not through labeling, criticism, or coercion. It's far better to provide the sparks of curiosity and help students see something interesting in their studies than attempt to motivate them by threats.

Rewarding students is also a form of coercion. Teachers use all kinds of rewards, from gold stars to extra privileges. Hearing you've won something, or getting 100% on an exam can provide momentary joy. But as Alfie Kohn points out in *Punished by Rewards*, students who do not get the reward can feel punished, even though no punishment was intended. (As I type this, my high school senior daughter is telling her mom about the anger of parents of high-achieving students in her class whose children *did not* get chosen as valedictorian!) Worse, rewards and punishments place the student at the mercy of the reward and the rewarder—students wind up doing the right thing for the wrong reason. Some say this is preparation for a world of work that rewards productivity and compliance. Yes, this may be the case in the workplace, but when students are driven by external rewards and not by their innate curiosity, engagement, or interest, they are not at their best as learners. Gifted educator Dr. Bob Smilovitz (1996) said, "As an educator, I nurture. I do not seek nor want allegiance and loyalty to my ideas. I wield a baton and not a hammer."

Rewarding students is never as beneficial as attributing: helping students build real, inner self-confidence over the long haul. Attributions ensure that students will continue to do well, not for the reward, but because *they have identified and internalized what makes them successful or unsuccessful.* To repeat: Attributing gives good information to the student, and gives useful information: "You did well on the project because you and Simon put a lot of effort into it." In other words, they have empowered themselves by recognizing that by their simple effort, they can accomplish much.

But it does not stop with self-empowerment. We teachers should not be shy about encouraging students to emulate good teachers, to empower others as well. Michael Umphrey (1996) said that when teaching children, we should "teach them to be teachers." Not professional teachers necessarily,

> but citizens of the kingdom of hope who believe that others can become better and more powerful creatures than they are and that such a becoming would be a good thing and that most people, when they can see, will freely choose such a course.

Umphrey concludes that the best teaching is when we lead students to freely choose what is wonderful. However, too many teachers still subscribe to a belief in coercion and control. According to Umphrey,

> (This leads) to faith in manipulation, deception, and intimidation. . . . The goal of control is control, but the goal of teaching is freedom. A teacher gives away the best that he or she has been given. Teaching authority wants the student to become the teacher's equal.

To hope for others to be our equal, and even to surpass us, is the essence of faith, and of humility, honesty, and love.

To repeat: If what is truly good is offered as one of the choices, students will freely choose it. Our job as teachers is decidedly not to rigidly identify exactly what our students must learn, and demand they learn it. Our job as teachers is to work as hard as we can *to offer as choices what is truly good, and not to feel unworthy of that lofty undertaking*. Who is to decide what is good? *Ultimately, each student selects his or her favorite flowers, but it is each teacher who provides the bouquets.*

13

Checking Your Compass

Four Checklists For Self-Assessment

COMPASS ASSESSMENT

The current fad of accountability, and its emphasis on standardized test scores, is giving assessment a bad reputation. Assessment is not a vulgar term. In fact, teachers each day make more assessments, and evaluation-related decisions than any other professional. Teachers assess students and self-assess their own work many, many times during their days, weeks, and careers. We assess how we teach: what could have been done better, differently, or not at all. When it comes to using the Compass, the form of self-assessment is a little different. It's not so much about identifying specific teaching practices (giving too much or too little homework, calling on the same students, etc.), but more about a teacher's feelings, attitudes, and aspirations. These are, in many ways, shown by your behavior as a teacher, and they affect teaching and learning far more powerfully than, say, a teacher's score on a standardized test. The Compass points and indicators describe the ways we *show ourselves to our students.* Hence, the Compass has a greater, and real, impact upon students than any content you are teaching. Students will recall how they felt in your classroom far longer than they will remember algebraic equations or the major exports of Mexico. Compass points show us what students will most strongly retain from our teaching. As I experienced with my classmates at our reunion many years after we had an inspirational teacher whose strong point of Love affected each of her students, the Compass points *stay with your students for a lifetime.*

Compass Checklist Instructions

There are several ways to use the Compass checklists. You can use the checklists on your own, by yourself. Or, you can use the checklists with a partner, perhaps a teacher colleague. Partners can provide feedback as well as advice to each other. Partners can serve as models to each other as well. The checklists can also be used within a group format, where several teachers meet, work together, and outline ways that Compass points serve to make their contact with students most beneficial. The group can serve the same functions as partners; that is, provide its members with feedback, guidance, and modeling.

In the checklists on pages 68 to 74, each point includes indicators, which are markers: simple statements that highlight one aspect of a Compass point. They are points of reflection, allowing us to give concrete shape and form to our efforts to be our best teacher. Indicators are best approached in the following manner:

Reflecting on each indicator, try to be an objective self-observer of your teaching, not too critical or too lenient, but straightforward and honest. As you look over the checklists, think about how each indicator describes you—what you do—as a teacher. Check the box in the "Yes" column if that indicator accurately describes your teaching behavior. (Note: You may *value* a certain item, but check "Yes" only if that item actually reflects the reality of your situation.) Check "Sorta" if that quality "sort of," sometimes, or moderately describes your teaching behavior. In a few cases, you may need to check "No," if that quality is not part of your teaching behavior.

If you have a trusted confidant, that person could provide a useful second opinion, helping you to see those indicators in which you are strong, and those indicators on which you need to work. Indeed, these checklists lend themselves well to being used by small groups of teachers, as bases for discussion.

Example: For instance, think about the first indicator: I "am here for my students." "Of course I am!" you may reply. And yes, you can add "I'm certainly not teaching for the money!" Indeed, some indicators are a quick "yes," but many are not. It's important not to dwell too long on each indicator. For each, check the "Yes," "Sorta," or "No" box and move on to the next indicator. Finally, note that at the end of each of the four lists, you can add indicators for each Compass point. These can be indicators that are unique to your teaching situation, and/or indicators you feel are important, yet missing from the checklist.

When you have finished the four checklists, look them over once more. See on which points you rated highest—those are your strong points. Conversely, see which Compass point needs strengthening.

North Checklist: Humility Indicators	Yes	Sorta	No
Toward the Compass point of Humility, I			
Am here for my students	☐	☐	☐
Reflect upon, plan for, and teach what is beneficial for my students	☐	☐	☐
Involve students in planning, in the life of our classroom	☐	☐	☐
Am able to admit when I am wrong	☐	☐	☐
Am prepared for my classes	☐	☐	☐
Take advantage of teachable moments	☐	☐	☐
Work each day to become my best teacher possible	☐	☐	☐
Use my power as a teacher wisely	☐	☐	☐
Provide affirmation for myself, my colleagues, and my students	☐	☐	☐
Additional Humility indicators are			

_____

_____

East Checklist: Honesty Indicators	Yes	Sorta	No
Toward the Compass point of Honesty, I			
Believe that all my students can and will be successful	☐	☐	☐
Treat all my students fairly; I involve all students	☐	☐	☐
Trust my good judgment when it comes to my students	☐	☐	☐
Teach my students that their own appraisal of their work is more important than anyone else's assessments of their work	☐	☐	☐
Work at being successful as a teacher	☐	☐	☐
Reflect upon my teaching, change what must be changed, and keep what works well	☐	☐	☐
Dialogue with my colleagues in a reflective way	☐	☐	☐
Encourage students to speak up for justice, not just when their self-interest is at stake	☐	☐	☐

Give students opportunities to revise their work	☐	☐	☐
Provide immediate and specific feedback to students	☐	☐	☐
Share my enthusiasm with my students and encourage students to share their enthusiasm	☐	☐	☐
Monitor students' work over time and expect students to self-monitor	☐	☐	☐
Use good assessments to inform my instruction	☐	☐	☐

Additional Honesty indicators are

_____

_____

South Checklist: Love Indicators	Yes	Sorta	No
Toward the Compass point of Love, I			
Know my students by name and as individuals	☐	☐	☐
Respect my students' parents and families and their cultural traditions and values	☐	☐	☐
Love even my students who act up or who are unpleasant or rude to me or to others	☐	☐	☐
Guard students' dignity in my classroom and teach my students how to safeguard their dignity and the dignity of others	☐	☐	☐
Avoid harshness and "crime-and-punishment" dealings	☐	☐	☐
Look at students when I speak to them and hear what they are saying	☐	☐	☐

Orient students toward each other	☐	☐	☐
Encourage students' framing the good in their day	☐	☐	☐
Actively plan for incorporating something joyful into my teaching	☐	☐	☐

Additional Love indicators are

_____

_____

West Checklist: Faith Indicators	Yes	Sorta	No
Toward the Compass point of Faith, I			
Use my power to empower students	☐	☐	☐
Hold clear but reasonable expectations for my students	☐	☐	☐
Believe all students can be—*and will be*—successful in my classroom	☐	☐	☐
Teach students about the *reasons* for their success, and orient them toward seeing for themselves	☐	☐	☐
Work at becoming a better listener . . . and a lesser talker	☐	☐	☐
Teach my students how to develop their inner teacher by listening to others, to me, and to themselves	☐	☐	☐
Am a teacher, not a judge	☐	☐	☐
Accept my students for who they are, today, right now	☐	☐	☐

Help students understand reasons for success or failure in school	☐	☐	☐
Avoid disengaged *laissez-faire* teaching approaches	☐	☐	☐
Trust my students and show that trust by my behavior	☐	☐	☐

Additional Faith indicators are

_____

_____

14

Putting It All Together

O nce you have gone through the various checklists, you should have a fairly clear idea of your Compass points of strength and weakness. On a daily and/or weekly basis, *reflect* on those Compass points. In addition, try to see new components for each of the four points *for yourself.* What are some of the key understandings that *you* take away from each of the Compass points? What new understandings have you gained?

Last, be secure in the knowledge that you have within yourself the most wonderful opportunity to bring about learning, and a love of learning, in other human beings. Our children and adolescents need *real* human beings as their teachers far more than they need well-trained technicians or slick educational specialists. In a world that—for the sake of control and conformity—is rapidly moving to minimize the uniqueness of every child (and every teacher), we owe it to ourselves and those we teach to uphold what it is about us human beings that really matters: the wisdom within us that is but a reflection of a deeper and profound Wisdom.

References

Aczell, A. D. (2001). *The riddle of the compass: The invention that changed the world.* New York: Harcourt.

benShea, N. (1990). *Jacob the baker.* New York: Ballantine.

Gribetz, J. (1997). *Wise words: Jewish thoughts and stories through the ages* (p. 204). New York: William Morrow.

Gulen, F. (2004). *Fethullah Gulen's Web site.* Retrieved February 14, 2004, from the World Wide Web: http://en.fgulen.com/a.page/life/as.a.teacher/p813.html

Hillel. *Mishnah 14, Pirkei Avot (The Ethics of the Fathers).* Retrieved March 2, 2004, from the World Wide Web: http://www.hillel.org/hillel/newhille.nsf

Holt, J. (1964). *How children fail.* New York: Pitman.

Kohl, H. (1994). *"I won't learn from you" and other thoughts on creative maladjustment.* New York: New Press.

Kohn, A. (1993). *Punished by rewards.* Boston: Houghton Mifflin.

Krishnamurti, J. (1953). *Education and the significance of life.* San Francisco: Harper & Row.

Ordway, R. (2004, February 7). Bangor teacher leaves legacy of kind humility. *Bangor* [Maine, U.S.A.] *Daily News.* Retrieved March 5, 2004, from the World Wide Web: http://www.bangornews.com/editorialnews/printarticle.cfm/ID/416842

Ruskin, J. (1885). *Time and tide, by Weare and Tyne: Twenty-five letters to a working man of Sunderland on the laws of work, by John Ruskin* (p. 8). New York: John W. Lovell.

Smilovitz, R. (1996). *If not now, when? Education, not schooling.* Kearney, NE: Morris.

Umphrey, M. (1996, September). A teacher's faith. *Holistic Education Review.* Retrieved February 24, 2004, from the World Wide Web: http://www.edheritage.org/articles/faith.htm

U.S. Department of Defense. (2002). *European area district teachers of the year.* Department of Defense Education Activity (DoDEA). Retrieved March 5, 2004, from the World Wide Web: http://www.odedodea.edu/teachers/toy02/european.htm

**CORWIN
PRESS**

The Corwin Press logo—a raven striding across an open book—represents the union of courage and learning. Corwin Press is committed to improving education for all learners by publishing books and other professional development resources for those serving the field of K–12 education. By providing practical, hands-on materials, Corwin Press continues to carry out the promise of its motto: **"Helping Educators Do Their Work Better."**